BUTTERFLY
METAMORPHOSI

Near Death Experience is a part of life. Earth is a brief journey, a learning place for something far greater than we can imagine.
We are loved unconditionally and have a higher purpose than mere existence. Be at peace for there are greater things to come.

JILL ROSIER ASTALL

Balboa Press books may be ordered through booksellers or by contacting:

Balboa Press
A Division of Hay House
1663 Liberty Drive
Bloomington, IN 47403
www.balboapress.com.au
1 (877) 407-4847

[Scripture quotations are from] Revised Standard Version of the Bible, copyright © 1946, 1952, and 1971 National Council of the Churches of Christ in the United States of America. Used by permission. All rights reserved worldwide.

ISBN: 978-1-5043-2023-8 (sc)
ISBN: 978-1-5043-2024-5 (e)

Print information available on the last page.

Balboa Press rev. date: 01/06/2020

BALBOA.PRESS
A DIVISION OF HAY HOUSE

BUTTERFLY METAMORPHOSIS

BY JILL ROSIER ASTALL

(AUTHOR OF "ART VERSUS THERAPY)

O

"WHEN LOVE BECKONS – FOLLOW HIM…..THOUGH HIS WAYS ARE HARD…AND WHEN HIS WINGS ENFOLD YOU, YIELD TO HIM….THOUGH THE SWORD HIDDEN AMONG HIS PINIONS MAY WOUND YOU."

KAHIL GIBRAN

DEDICATED TO THE SOULS LOST THROUGH OUR
FRAGILE EXISTENCE ON THIS EARTH

ACKNOWLEDGEMENT

Thanks for continued support from:

"Revival Centres International Box Hill"
Michael la Greca & Members of the Community.

In memory of those lost in Earthquake 2016.

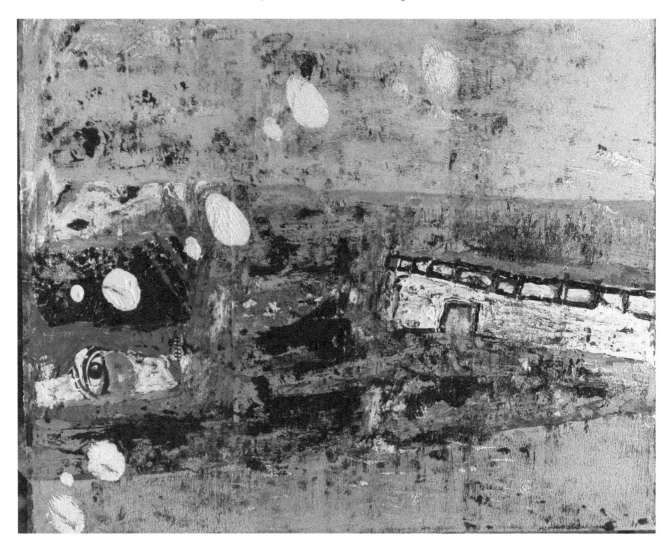

"MEXICO" - Acrylic Painting/Collage by Jill Rosier Astall

DEPARTURE

Heaven is only one cloud away
Look, there's the turret
Blue and sky white
Stained glass reflecting
Cars, dogs, people
Horizons like stanza's of prose
Blue sky white
Don't look down
Go with it
Lifting lightly
You're in the blue wispy cloud
Breathe
Nearly there
We'll land soon
On a super moon
Eclipsing all you've known before
No
Don't cry
You haven't lost anything
You've punched through the stratosphere
Intense gravitation

Embrace the energy
Of the blood moon
And the buried souls of Mexico
Transcend through white vapour
Wafting in azure skies
Welcome
Come
Find peace
Rest
No, no
Don't look back
All is gone
But look up
Here
By your side
The others come to welcome you
For you, my love, are home

"HOMESICK" Wardrobe Reflections Acrylic Painting/Collage /Digital Photography by Jill Rosier Astall

REFLECTIONS

Homesick
The flight of birds
To homelands gone
Carrying bonds of love
Memories vague
I can no longer see their faces
I can no longer hear them speak
Alone
Castaway
Of no use
The last bauble, broken
Decrepit
Vacuous
Shut up
Shut out
Void
Below
A painting of a nude
Briefly fertile
Throw it out
It's had its day

"FAITH" Digital Photography/Oil Painting by Jill Rosier Astall

METAPHOR

"Drinkies on Thursday" he writes
Followed by a guilty conscience
"I love Jill"
Intention
Admittance
The wardrobe vomits out
Tasteless indiscretion
Of learning how to moonwalk
And sweet talk
Another woman
Older
Bolder
Desperate
Love your babies
Keep them close
The time will come
When you are not necessary
But did you have to
Have coffee with the blonde nurse
While I was pushing out your daughter?

"SOULFREE" Acrylic Painting/Collage by Jill Rosier Astall

LOVE

Does not bargain
Nor negotiate terms
Is not a business deal
Is not conditional
Is given freely
Openly
Naturally
Without competition
Or justification
Without manipulation
Or self-gratification
But with
Open delight
And Surprise

"SUBURBAN GARDEN OF EDEN" Acrylic Painting/Collage by Jill Rosier Astall

THE DEEP AND SHALLOW

He loiters
He does
The one with teeth
That rip my flesh
He lies
In shallows
His eyes darting
In the murk
Between two rocks
I see them glint and flicker
One snap he takes
To catch my tail
My flesh like his
All scales
Broken.
Above planet sun
She burns my earth
Wispy reeds sway
Waves lap
And he rules
The deep and shallow

"FOOD CHAIN" Acrylic Painting/Printmaking by Jill Rosier Astall

DECEPTION

I thought one day I'd have a husband
I thought one day I'd have a home
I dreamed of raising up a family
Never dreamt I'd be alone
I thought that I would live in comfort
I thought I would be warm and safe
I dreamt of privilege and of love
Not of violence and fist in glove
I dreamt of writing this sad memory
I dreamt of kindness, warm and true
Ironic that the world has dealt me a more realistic aspic view

"HOMELESSNESS" Acrylic Painting/Digital Photography by Jill Rosier Astall

HOME SWEET... CAVE

While the big boys play with their big toys
The missiles make an unholy noise
Bombing areas of concern
We the public are to learn
Why saving people ends in death
Of children, elderly, women and pets
Roads blocked to hospitals and vets
Masks preventing inhalation of air
Chemicals, fires, bombings and despair

To go from home to here to roam

WHERE?

"THE ROCK" Acrylic Painting by Jill Rosier Astall

NOT ONE TO SHARE A CONVERSATION

And we did meet upon the stairs
The music throbbing
Couples clutching hopefully
An infantile insult
Interrupted my conversation
A smug jibe
"You don't look like arties"
A smartarse judgement
With pious expression
Followed by
A paedophiles approach
Of offered lollies
A non-stop diatribe
Of endless self-gratuitous
Chatter/a mummy's boy/a weird shirt.

"INTERGALACTIC RELATIONSHIPS" Acrylic Painting/
Sculptured Mask/Oil Painting/Collage by Jill Rosier Astall

THE REASONS WHY

Sit and listen to me talk
Admire my witty repertoire
Notice my enticing walk
I've often thought the most outspoken
Rather akin to a record broken
Mannerisms coarse and vacuous
Hackneyed comments oh so tactless
Innuendo without base
Rumour spread remiss of taste
A simple term meant so kindly
Now so public just remind me
Never to associate
And those who think that they are
GREAT Often sublimate the TRUTH

"LIFEFORCE" Acrylic/Collage Painting by Jill Rosier Astall

MOONLIT COCOON

Mangled we are
From roughness of handling
Pecked at by beaks of pterodactyl
Proportions
Bedraggled we feel
From icy gusts
Of sleet, rain and torrent.
What resplendent satin darkness
Shall envelope us
Emerging victorious
Over raucous elemental factions.
Wait beauty
One more earth rotation
Grant us reason to sway
Beauty doth wait
Just one more season
Whilst my silken coat
Remains intact
No penetration shall enact
Nor shall it claim
The jewel within
For I am but pupae to spin

"PARISIAN ARCADE" Digital Photography/Parisian Street/
Oil Painting/Collage/Sculptured Mask by Jill Rosier Astall)

ARCHAIC LOVE

He views with scorn the plight
Of the lost and forlorn
The humanoids must flee their cocoon
Before starkness-light of full moon
Not a moment to waste
Haste haste.
One is gone who can't be saved
Hanging from a balustrade.
In floral dress of deep primrose
And pointed shoes
Her life to lose.
Two will jump from windowsills
The fall too great but preferable still
To granting his unquestionable will
To dominate his gentle mate.
Too late too late

The angel she appears above
To save them from archaic love
Where woman is attached to man
Unevolved, misogynistic
Brutal and so egotistic

"PEACE" Acrylic Painting by Jill Rosier Astall

REPRODUCTION

Humanity VS. Nature

A butterfly emerges from pupae state, fully equipped and independent, with the ability to fly. A human baby does not. Realizing this it cries copiously with great umbrage at being removed from its cocoon with or without force. A butterfly can be born damaged with one wing deformed or a feeler bent and twisted. It must cope on it's own in a world not known for its compassion towards those with disability which compounds the likelihood of being consumed by a ravenous bird, desperate to feed her chicks. Kill or be killed. In that context humans can be just as Machiavellian by destroying another females' spawn or invading her nest. Survival disposes of the weakest whether animal, mineral, vegetable or human. The latter predisposed to equal capacity for harm to others for its' own ascension. A state of competition v. compassion. Take weeds for instance. They tend to takeover in a rather presumptuous manner, assuming they are due more turf. But of what purpose are they? Only to be outranked by a sudden, glorious burst of jonquil, or ravishing display of petunia or phlox. Weeds are in essence common and plain.

The butterfly lives for one day. A human baby has the capacity to reach one hundred with or without deformity at any stage of its existence. Most humans of higher principle are less inclined to destructive measures. Moral code dictates affability, resourcefulness and a respect for others. It is a two way street between parent-child, boss-worker and doctor-patient. A mentor can guide others with compassion and support providing their goals are altruistic and they themselves are backed with supportive professionals.

The patient can attack the healer/counsellor/tutor/parent or even self-harm in cases of severe psychotic episodes which are becoming more prevalent in our society, tragically. Children are hot-housed earlier whilst parents work to earn a living or follow a career they are not willing or able to release. Whilst day-care can be enjoyable to some it is difficult to presume the type of day a child has had should they not be old enough to tell you. Illness is also a concern at a younger age as interaction with many germs is highly likely. Babies are completely vulnerable. It is confusing the justifications made by parents to pay for expensive day-care services which make budgeting tougher. Friends who put both their sons in day-care so the parents could earn a higher lifestyle and bigger home have expressed concern that the children learn to be aggressive and competitive earlier. Hence when they are assimilated into Kindergarten as three year olds behavioural patterns form manifesting a repeat of survival tactics learned in day-care centres. We are all victims of learned behavioural patterns. No different to animals fighting for survival in a world where parents can throw us out of the nest at any stage.

In witnessing a group of Kindergarten children there were definitive groups of natural selection. One group was "The Pirate Group" made up of five or so boys armed with tree branches, rocks and playground equipment which they would hurl at friends. If no weapon could be found it became paramount to wrestle a friend to the ground. This group generally spread itself further in a conquest to exert supremacy by trampling over sand castles being designed by quieter and more co-operative attendees building a utopia. Like a hive of bees the gang then descended upon three or four girls and two boys enjoying a make believe tea ceremony, who exclaimed indignantly, "You are not invited to this tea party. Go away". Ah yes, the hierarchy of society were already ensconced in property management.

Two of the boys then ran furiously into a jungle gym and were taken immediately to the nearest hospital to receive stitches.

One little girl was playing alone by the garden, digging a hole for a new plant purchased by the Kindergarten Staff. Others were whispering and gossiping and forming social cliques.

A quiet boy was sitting in a used dinghy, no doubt dreaming of fishing as a serious girl walked around the chaos and mayhem to approach the tree behind him. The comfort of tree and beauty of nature and solitude relaxed her expression and she noticed the boy sitting quietly in his boat. Ten minutes later they were pals, rowing the deep seas and oblivious to all else.

In comparison to butterflies, humans have a longer life span to create or destroy and experience this planet, for better or worse. It is comforting to know we can leave the planet for a time during dream state or NDE (Near Death Experience) which is really just like day dreaming on a summer's day at the beach and we've fallen into a sort of slumber until someone accidentally kicks sand in our face and we are rudely interrupted. However we do not expect such a rude awakening in the seclusion of our own bedroom. Confronting.

"DREAM STATE/ASCENSION TO TEMPLE: TICKETS PLEASE"
Acrylic & Calligraphy Ink Painting by Jill Rosier Astall

"I awake to find a being of light sitting on my chest. It is solid and heavy and its eyes are of another world, brilliant and piercing. I cannot breathe, which is not unusual for me as I have just recovered from another acute asthma attack. My immediate reaction to this presence is fear and discomfort.

What is it doing? Am I dreaming? My chest feels so heavy. Get off me! I try to scream but nothing comes out. I am paralysed. I literally cannot move my arms to push it off or defend myself. My brain tells me to struggle but my body does not respond to the silent directive. The "being" has frozen me.

25

As I look into its eyes to try to make sense of what is happening I feel a solid shaft of light enter my body, my emotions, my soul. The light is tactile, concrete. Then, as if conveying some ephemeral power, immense feelings of love are transmitted. I have never known such love. It is divine. It is peace. It is bliss. An alien being is sitting on my chest sending me divine love. My nineteen year old brain tells me this can't be so but my body has never known such peace.

It lifts off me and moves to my bedroom door. Half way across the floor it transforms into a youngish, slight man wearing old-fashioned pleated trousers and a fob watch tucked into a pocket on his vest. I wonder if it is my grandfather but he is too short and it is someone I have not seen before. Is it a guardian angel? A relative who has passed? Am I dying? Its presence is calming. It has shown me a doorway to another world by reaching its arm out to welcome me. I do not have earthly language to describe this experience but it has been calming. I am unable to make sense of my manifestation nor source the vocabulary to define it. The need to call out to my parents is gone. I check to see if I am awake by scratching my arm. Ouch! I AM awake!

The next morning the scratches are there. So it did happen! I check my asthma medication to see if I took the wrong dosage. No, all is well. I do not tell my parents. I do not tell anyone.

Years later a friend relays a similar experience she had and I feel lucky that my NDE was positive and loving. She tells me her experience was very frightening and somewhat reminiscent of "The Nightmare" painted by Fuseli.

"I was asleep. Woke up with the feeling something was sucking out all my breath until I couldn't breathe at all. I was paralysed. I literally couldn't move. It was crushing me and I couldn't breathe. A Teacher/Parent is emailing me about her daughter. She is not doing well in Maths. And the mother is blaming me. I think it's a sign I should get the hell out of this school. Who do I report this too?"

So we establish we need a trip to Qi in Elsternwick and purchase some crystals for protection and general well-being and any other excuse to splurge.

The school gave no acknowledgement of her new grandchild so I completed drawings and a painting in honour of her extended lineage. We have walked a similar path and found a natural camaraderie in a school that unfortunately prides itself in spreading insecurity amongst staff and vicious backstabbing. Combined with weak Leadership the students and staff suffer. Shame. But bonds are formed under such conditions in this bigger playground as adults and we form alliances naturally. We have the sitting in a boat under the tree type friendship. Purveying the silly behaviour of our playmates and exhausted from game-playing tactics of both verbal and physical violence amongst our fellow humanoids who are now adults, supposedly. Insecurity underlies attack on any level, unless it is self-defence. Survival mechanisms kick in and response is quick. Verbally one can choose to educate or reason with an aggressor but when you are being choked the only recourse is to physically defend yourself even if it does not stand up in a court of law. Some children who have not attended Kindergarten at all find socialization difficult as they do not master the skills required. Narcissistic, Sociopathic or even worse Psychopathic tendencies can evolve. The debate rests on nature/nurture causality.

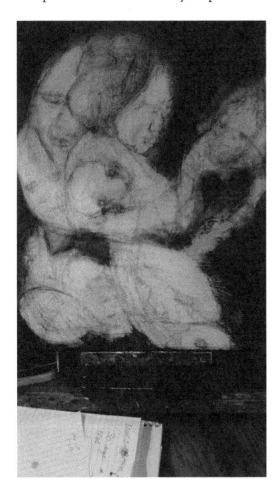

"Lineage Images" Acrylic Painting and supportive sketches/plan by the Jill Rosier Astall

27

Melbourne University has also documented that once people experience an NDE event, they never see the world in the same way again. They are more likely to divorce as nothing really compares with witnessing the extreme shaft of love and life. It is an inexplicable experience that transcends life on Earth literally.

Some relate NDE's to proof of alien sightings.

In 1966 there was a mass UFO sighting in a suburb in Westall/Clayton South. This is not far from where I live in Carnegie.

On 6th April, 1966 early in the morning two hundred school students witnessed an unidentified flying object. This is the largest UFO sighting in Australia. Later some of the students shared their experience with one student running into the classroom shouting "There's a flying saucer outside!"

The classmates went to the corner of the schoolyard to see. There were two saucers, one on the bottom and one turned upside down on the top. She saw three. They were hovering over the trees and then went down into the trees and disappeared for a minute or two, then rose back up, sort of banked on its side and then took off at a thousand miles per hour. Many people of course are sceptical but the children described what they saw and it was uniform.

In two foot high grass was a perfect circle of flattened grass. There were three distinct impressions where the grass had been penetrated down to the dirt.

The following day it was cordoned off and a military officer ordered people off the area. So clearly something did happen for that precaution to be enforced.

Nine News reported the event on the 6pm bulletin.

Interestingly, the film canister is now empty in archives and witnesses believe there has been a cover-up.

I have spoken to witnesses in the area and they tell of one student being rushed to hospital due to the shock of the event and another who verifies the sighting as reported by the press as he was a student there at the time who witnessed the entire event.

From my bedroom window on the second floor I have a direct view of the area and now often see what seem to be weather balloons moving in a strange manner, directly up and down and then moving in a formulated pattern. They are hovering and not simply travelling through the area like a plane or helicopter. Curious shapeshifting phenomenon.

"THE EMPTY CONGREGATION" Photography & Painting by Jill Rosier Astall

"CRUMBLE: NOTRE DAME 1" Acrylic Painting by Jill Rosier Astall

"CRUMBLE: NOTRE DAME 2" Acrylic Painting by Jill Rosier Astall

Acrylic Painting showing burning of Rose window, Paris and gargoyles tumbling from above, thus illuminating evil whilst the Butterfly represents metamorphosis. As I write this two wild possums are chasing each other across my roof and throwing themselves recklessly onto a nearby wattle tree that has grown exponentially high. The possums resemble falling gargoyles with their enlarged, bulbous eyes and frantic lunging to catch each other, or attempt screeching reproduction on a slippery overhanging branch just outside my window. The balcony is a favourite post for them to rest or oversee the world they inhabit. At this time of night it is definitely their world, with claws capable of ripping open skin in one swipe. There have been aggressive tussles on my balcony and pieces of fruit left kindly are often cause for vicious battles. My cat alarmed by such aggression, looks pleadingly for me to stop the fracas but there is nothing that could tempt my interference. They inhabit our space with wildness so demonic and eyes piercing the night, if they do meet up with humans reckless enough to invade their territory possums would be the victors in any battle. A nightmare situation of evil spirits pervades the springtime gallivanting of Australian wild possums.

On a human scale, do spirit communicate with us during dreams? This has been documented during REM sleep studies and is termed Paradoxical Sleep.

Sleep brainwaves (REM) patterns are similar to when a person is awake. Visual neurons fire the same when awake. Eyes dart back and forth and heart rate, blood pressure and respirations fluctuate up and down. Sometimes called Paradoxical Sleep the physiology is close to that of being awake but brainstem blocks all muscle movement. Rem time increases with each cycle of sleep.

We have four to six dreams every night and our subconscious creates these stories from our current state of mind and emotional state.

In the 1900's, Freud believed dream was a result of our deepest anxieties and desires or connected to repressed childhood memories or obsessions. Precognitive dream shows the dreamer a vision of the future and some dreams are actual warnings. Others are validations. Is it a message from spirit or just a coincidence? In waking life it's déjà vu.

Hypnagogic is when the mind is not asleep or awake. REM is deepest sleep. Many people go into meditative state to "meet" spirit guides.

It is known sleep paralysis can cause a person to hallucinate. Medications, stress, over-tiredness and alcohol consumption can have the same effect. Does scientific explanation really explain all phenomenon?

Lucid Dreaming is when there is awareness it is a dream. This can be used effectively by the medical field to treat anxiety and PTSD (Post Traumatic Stress Disorder).

Temporary paralysis relaxes the muscles via REM sleep and vivid dreams ensue. Sometimes a person wakes up too early, is conscious but unable to move or speak. Some report seeing figures in the room or at the foot of the bed or in doorways. They feel heaviness on their chest or a choking sensation. Terrifying sleep paralysis, sleep-deprived, stressed, narcolepsy or sleep apnoea can be associated with negative spirits or psychic attack.

So how do we tell the difference between a dream and a visitation? There is usually a specific message from loved ones and the energy of love is manifested. A glowing light indicates divine presence and often emerges at a time of grief or loss of a loved one.

Consciousness is the common denominator.

So, does our consciousness live after we die? Our world is three dimensional. Some consider the 4th Dimension to be a bridge between physical and spiritual and therefore a higher form of consciousness. The 4th Dimension manifests astral travel and is not restricted to time.

In hindsight there are probably a number of explanations for my hallucinations that night. Doctors and scientists may describe it as a Near Death Experience, a reaction to meds or maybe before waking I stopped breathing. Scientists at my alma mater, Melbourne University, have measured and documented the sensations that patients feel when they have died and returned. They explain in technical terminology about the chemicals that surge through our brains before death and the physical reactions. Some people see past relatives, some see a white light or travel through a tunnel. Others recall life events or leave their bodies, looking down at the scene of their own floating soul.

Nurses witnessing the actual death of patients confirm these phenomena. An ex-student of mine from Japan told me her mother, a Doctor, sees black dust rising out of a dying patient at the very moment of death.

Was my experience a physical, scientific manifestation caused by a near death event or a reaction to drugs prescribed?

Or, was my experience divinely ordered. Was it spiritual or was it aliens? Was it both? Was it my angel? I do not deny my faith or the belief in a Higher Power. Faith has no need for proof. It is proven to you in daily life and the minutiae of our miraculous existence. If science can one day measure faith how will it prove it? By technical results from a machine that spurts out complex formula? I prefer to accept firsthand experience via medical staff who have witnessed phenomenon.

Some search via religious doctrine to connect to higher power or to know God. I have witnessed many. The message somewhat distorted to suit the historical belief system of family or that which we inherited via genealogy. As a child I insisted my parents take me to Sunday School at St. Mary's Church of England, Caulfield. The sermons and hymns were traditional, repetitive and related to studies of Biblical Text. I also had my confirmation as a teenager at the same church however, the Minister at the time confused my childhood friend and I and we were subsequently confirmed as the other person. Biblically, does that mean we are interchangeable? Did our souls swap over at the moment of confirmation? Can anyone confirm that please? I won prizes at Sunday School. In the early days my parents would kneel either side of the bed and say their prayers. I thought this was magic. I gave my father a list of the Ten Commandments from Sunday School for Father's Day one year. He was a little perplexed. Mum couldn't stop laughing. As an adult I now see the irony. Times were secure and predictable. Not now.

As a teenager I went to a Methodist School where the structure was somewhat "fire and brimstone" with lots of singing. I won a prize in Year Ten for receiving 100% in Scripture.

Being a humoristic student my friends took great delight in teasing me for ages after that!

According to His Holiness the Dalai Lama in "The Art of Happiness" there are different levels of spirituality. Religious beliefs are shared by so many people of different dispositions.

He has been known to report the need for five billion religions to cater for five billion people. "I believe that each individual should embark upon a spiritual that is best suited to his or her mental disposition, natural inclination, temperament, belief, family and cultural background." (p. 294 Ch. 15)

Indeed, in Mesopotamia when Noahs Ark ran adrift all religions in surrounding countries sighted Noah and the Ark. Reporters and journalists all had a different view of the occasion. Scientists declared the Ark was a "floating iceberg in the shape of a boat/ship". (ABC documentary/Joanna Lumley).

Religion should be a remedy to help reduce the conflict and suffering in the world, not another source of conflict. Freedom of choice should be respected to avoid the oxymoron of a Holy War. To many people God and Religion are anathema to their lifestyle. So be it. Live and let live. We are not clones to convert those of different persuasions nor do we have the right or authority to override or disrespect another's path. Atheists have a difficult time accepting the existence of any form of God whatsoever and seek to concentrate on the negatives of belief systems as being viable under any context. Almost as if believers are weak individuals, easily lead by the hierarchy, or simple people, brainwashed by cultism. Witches were burnt at the stake, seers deemed possessed by ignorance and fear of any people appearing to have higher source to knowledge.

In court one must swear on the Bible. This is somewhat of a dichotomy. Galatians 3:11-14 professes that "we might receive the promise of the Spirit through faith". And "Now it is evident that no man is justified before God by the law; for "He who through Faith is righteous shall live"; but "the law does not rest on faith". "Christ redeemed us from the curse of the law" so that we "might receive the promise of the Spirit through faith."

23-27 "Now before faith came we were confined under the law, kept under restraint until faith should be revealed. But now that faith has come, we are no longer under a custodian; for in Jesus Christ you are all sons of God, through faith. For as many of you as were baptized into Christ have put on Christ."

Personal relationship with God is not defined by not understanding principles of the law made by man, not God. One can be righteous but not justified by the faith of the law. God's grace is unconditional.

While attending a Methodist school, I went to a Uniting Church youth group. We all church hopped accepting the safety of socializing in a protected arena. Unexpected pregnancies and hushed rumours abounded. Terminations were experienced by some and the "go forth and multiply" factor ignored. It is ironic some parents happy with their adolescent daughters going to church were so incredibly unaware of the "goings on". Naive, in fact. So many delicious attendances at Rock concerts and Festival Hall. Bliss. I remember the responsible leader of our church youth group organizing an outing to see "Jesus Christ Superstar" that contained (via John English) a full frontal nude appearance on stage. Our leader had rather desperately smuggled in binoculars.

Biblical text went in one ear and out the other as we focused mainly on our attire, mini-skirts and lipstick. Nothing scriptural was challenged.

Later followed interest in Meditation and Studies of Buddhism at Melbourne University, the wearing of the obligatory caftans, Ishka apparel and after Graduating, teaching a particularly rowdy Year 10 class as Head of the Art Faculty at Siena College, Camberwell yoga was discovered with a colleague taking the same group of rowdy 10's. That year my students beat Melbourne Grammar in Art Moderation, my top student interviewed Ivan Durrant and I got pregnant with my first child. Here ended the career for a long, long time and I was swallowed up by suburbia, a dark and Gothic experience with the light of babies glowing pure love. It would have been easier if my Mum was still alive and I missed her so much. But life throws us curve balls, yes?

Here, church was just around the corner but rarely visited. Except for Christenings and Fetes. Here, women gathered to mull over the change from successful careers to domesticity. Slowly but surely, the educated amongst us forged our way back to work, either from monetary urgency, boredom, loneliness or mental sanity. Feminism wasn't mentioned. We were already doing it. Wages as Head of Faculty were equal. Principals were equally spread across schools and gender was non-specific.

It was a time of claiming equality. Or trying to. How fortunate to have aspired to escape the slavery of the previous generation and the mind-numbing domesticity. As Teachers we had the same hours as our children. As a sole parent it was exhausting doing all the work. No matter who you have around you, it is your life to live. Freedom to pursue your own interests and respect that in others. Life throws some curve balls but to aspire to achieve a dream is every person's right.

A strong religious faith can help more effectively with aging, personal crises and traumatic effects.

A study done by Ronna Casar Harris and Mary Amanda Dew found that heart transplant patients with strong religious beliefs have less difficulty coping with postoperative medical regimens and show better long-term physical and emotional health. When it gets beyond you, give it to God. Join that group that can help you bounce back and lift you up to higher source. I have felt that support. Beliefs can offer hope in the face of adversity, suffering and death.

Dr. Thomas Oxman and his colleagues at Dartmouth Medical School found that patients over the age of 55 who underwent open-heart surgery for coronary artery or heart valve diseases and who had taken refuge in their religious beliefs were ten times more likely to survive than those who did not. If it works why must the individual enter into a debate from the public realm re: the viability of Religion and the presence or existence of God Himself.

Miracles exist. Define miracle in your own terms. To cultivate stillness of mind is to bring happiness and peace. That state of being can cure illness, lower blood pressure, regulate tachycardia or create miracles inexplicable to medical staff. To think seriously about the real meaning of spiritual practices, is all about training your mind and your mental state, attitudes, psychological and emotional state and well-being.

It is a methodology of self control over thought processes via self-reflection.

"This too shall pass".

Teresa of Avila said:
Let nothing disturb you
Let nothing frighten you
All things pass away
God never changes
Patience obtains all things
He who has God lacks for nothing
God alone suffices

A man with a neurological condition caused by chronic use of anti-psychotic medication (Tandive dyskinesia) was waiting in a crowd for the Dalai Llama to attend a reception. He was heavily crushed by the crowd. The Dalai Llama broke free to talk to him, took his hand, patted it and stood silently nodding. The look of pain and agitation suddenly seemed to drain from his face and tears ran down his cheeks as a look of comfort and gladness appeared in the man's eyes.

Healing is also a common practice used by many in the congregation and throughout services. This Saturday I have two lovely people visiting me to pray for my health. I was diagnosed with Cardiomyopathy eight years ago. It was found by accident after my daughter was admitted to hospital. I had a heart attack and was rushed to Monash Medical Centre. My left ventricle was only working on 20%. I had MRI's and the Cardiologist suggested explorative surgery in case they found something else. Cardiomyopathy can be Idiopathic and simply go by itself. It can occur during times of high stress. I refused. Before entering the tunnel of the MRI machine I had been seeing flashes of blue light the night before. The male nurse and I had been talking about miracles and Archangel Michael. Blue light being a symbol of his presence. This gave me such peace and strength. I had a choice and need no validation what-so-ever from those who think it reckless. I believe we can be healed without medical intervention. I believe we can be healed by faith. Since the age of eighteen months I have had life-threatening asthma attacks. Adrenalin shots kept me alive. One year I missed eight months of school and was so weak I could not walk. My mother had to carry me to the bath, crying all the way there and back again she would say, "I can see your ribs sticking out"! They expected me to die and at one time I wanted to, collapsing with one massive attack and telling my Mum that I couldn't stay. She shook my pillow so hard I was denied a peaceful exit! I wasn't meant to go yet.

This is true service to God's healing powers and the soul often displays itself through being healed, witnessed by congregation or loved ones. How different is it to Medical Staff witnessing the healing of a dying patient or one declared dead, who then breathes again. In both cases miracle and divine intervention is a term used. Non acceptance of others belief systems is xenophobic in essence. Firsthand experience needs no proof. It simply is proof. No sign of life declared by surgeons cannot explain life re-appearing whilst on the trolley being pushed by staff to the morgue. Or, in some cases, bodies in the morgue coming back to life hours after being declared dead.

History can be proven by the finding of mass graves. Archaeologists excavating on Mount Zion in Jerusalem have uncovered evidence of the Babylonian conquest of the city, appearing to confirm a Biblical account of its destruction.

Academics from the University of North Carolina at Charlotte, made significant finds, including ash deposits, arrowheads and broken pieces of pots and lamps. The most surprising discovery, however, was an item of jewellery, which appears to be a tassel or earing with a bell-shaped upper portion.

Professor Shimon Gibson, Co-Director of the Universities Mount Zion Archaeological project, told CNN this year that the recovery of the rare piece of jewellery is the first time that archaeologists have uncovered signs of the "elites", thereby appearing to confirm Biblical descriptions of Jerusalem's wealth prior to the conquest in 587-586 BC.

Professor Gibson said jewellery is a rare find at conflict sites as warriors would normally steal it and melt it down.

It is a clear sign of the wealth of the inhabitants of the city at the time of the siege. While the items in isolation don't provide conclusive evidence of the Babylonian attack, the unique mix of artefacts leads researchers to believe they have uncovered direct evidence of the conquest which was led by the Neo-Babylonian King Nebuchadnezzar 11. There was significant loss of life when the city was razed to the ground. It also led to the destruction of King Solomon's Temple (a story recounted in the Old Testament's Second Book of Kings.

Orthodox Jews around the world commemorate the event every year on Tisha B'Au, an annual day of fasting and mourning, which this year took place on Sunday. The day which is regarded as the saddest in the Jewish Calendar, also marks the destruction of the Second Temple by Roman legions around 70 AD.

We are all to die eventually or sooner than expected. Fact. We are all fascinated by how, when and where this monumental event will take place. Did we worry before we were born? When were we conscious of life? There is timely death and untimely death. Mindfulness of death cannot be experienced by a foetus in utero. The definition of death in "The Path of Purification" (Visuddhi Magga) is: "Herein, death (marana) is the interruption of the life faculty included within a single becoming (existence)." Mindfulness of Death is the remembering or interruption of life faculty.

Development of this is via solitary retreat. Death will take place; the life faculty will be interrupted. There are mini-deaths.

Sorrow arises in death of an agreeable person, as in a mother, child or friend. Relief arises in the passing of a disagreeable person who may have been an enemy or hurt us in some way throughout their lifespan. The ease of a difficult relationship does not bring mourning but happiness. The death of a neutral person is merely a fact without emotion.

Death will take place and we are seldom in control of the methodology. Death can come with birth, sadly and there is no returning to the comfort of the womb. It is said the child chooses the mother.

Corpses have been declared dead as previously mentioned, and commenced breathing life hours later. Deemed "a miracle" or a fault of man's interpreted knowledge of science.

Destiny of the soul has no sign as there is no definition. Some die in a divine world and are reborn in the human world and vice-versa.

When consciousness dissolves, the world is dead. But fear not we may return. Death then becomes a pathway to a new realm and a reinvention of new life. All a learning process and soul journey. All things are possible and infinite. We are never alone as nothing is truly separate from our true being which is spirit. Animals have souls. Birds follow me and land on my balcony every morning. Crows land on the grass nearby giving me a knowing look of protection as I walk up the street. They do not fear me and I do not fear being pecked! I prefer the company of animal spirit to human spirit. I trust animals. Humans have agendas. Animals know who to trust. Whilst waiting for the bus to school a bird was shocked by a live wire and landed directly at my feet. I hid it in my school bag and went directly to the Science Lab. where my Science Teacher promised to put it under "the lights" for a while. At the end of the day it was sitting in a cage singing. It had been shocked by the overhanging livewire but had recovered with a bit of loving care.

I have always kept budgies (Budgerigars) delighting in their raucous personalities. The last budgie died after a long life and was in the corner of the cage, wings spread out as if she was flying and a divine expression of peace in her eyes. Very different to my first budgie, Joey, who was comically positioned in a classical dead-budgie pose, flat on her back and legs in the air. Still she looked peaceful, eyes closed and smiling. If that is possible.

I have had four beautiful cats and the one I have at the moment (Miss Lottie) is an angel. My children are grown and gone and I was depressed for six months adapting to the quiet and lack of comradeship we shared when they were younger. "Jill, you're depressed" said a close friend, "Get a cat, you've never NOT had one!" Luckily I was working with a girl whose cat had just birthed six kittens. To cut a long story short I removed "Miss Lottie" from squalid surroundings and she rules my life. She licks my tears. We are soul mates. She is famous on my facebook page and is a member of a "Cat Group" which shares the antics of Arty-friend cat owners. I am not bragging when I say she is praised by everyone she meets here at home and wins their hearts. I have cared for many overseas university students who adored her and she would greet them at the door with no fear of visitors.

As I get older and vaguer, she reminds me of daily tasks by standing near whatever needs to be done. First is her breakfast dish, next fresh grass from outside as she is an indoor cat and needs grass for her digestive system. Then she waits while I have breakfast and reminds me to empty her kitty litter by standing at the laundry door. Upstairs we go and she stays with me as I have a shower. We then make the bed which becomes play-time for her as she unmakes it for me by pushing off cushions. She likes ritual. If I go up the street she waits in the same spot until I return with shopping and "helps" me unpack. If I sit down anywhere, at anytime she jumps on my knee. Playtime starts when she drops toys at my feet. Being very intelligent she knows repeated phrases.

She can also sense when visitors have a "problem", whether that be anger-management or psychiatric conditions. She leaves the room and hides upstairs in my room. Her instincts are spot on. Animals can be more sensitive to illnesses in humans and their instincts astute. I used to raise money to provide support animals for people with disability or special needs. One phone call linked me to a gentleman who was clearly depressed. On speaking further he told me his wife had died and his dog was depressed too. His wife had suffered from cancer and sat in a chair for months, slowly getting weaker and weaker. The dog would sit next to her all day, his head on her knee. When she died he climbed onto her bed and refused to move. When I called the man was lying on the bed with the dog, crying. He had two cats which stayed outside for most of the day but came in for dinner. After his wife died the cats would try and get the dog off the bed but he refused to move. They had now given up and lay next to the dog all day. As the man relayed such a sad story I couldn't speak….a rare event! I too was crying. On hearing this the gentleman said, "Thank you for talking to me and understanding, please don't cry. You are doing such a good job. I love the cause. Please take a $1,000.00 donation from me and my pets to help someone else." My boss had been listening to the call and as I looked up, he too had tears in his eyes. How beautiful is life when we utilize our higher selves by caring for one another. How beautiful are the souls of animals when they comfort their humans. How beautiful is life when we comfort any animal needing kindness. How sad when they pass on.

Two days after my 3rd cat died my daughters and I, all living in separate homes, felt a cat jump on the bed as we were drifting off to sleep. At first I thought it was a memory imprint until they called and relayed the visitation on their beds. "Mr. Kitty", a giant of a cat, was saying his goodbyes. We will meet again, beautiful one.

"THE SOURCE OF ALL UNDERSTANDING" SOPHIA AND BAPHOMET.
Acrylic Painting/Collage with traditional varnish by Jill Rosier Astall

Sophia is referred to in Biblical Text as the Divine Mother of wisdom. Hebrew in essence she receives only three lines. Baphomet and The Abyss discusses the philosophy of The Templars.

"THE OXYMORON OF A HOLY WAR"
By Jill Rosier Astall

The Knights Templar
Offer the Sabbatic goat
History rotates
On Russian roulette
We spin
Out of Control
Into China
Where nothing is finer
Except the U.S. of A and Carolina
The God's of Egypt
Safe in their sarcophagi
Play eye spy with my little eye
And sigh
History repeats
Whilst war deletes
Humanity with one button of
Insanity sending you and I into
Infinity
Stock up on the Angels Heaven
The power game has rung
Its final siren

Sophia's mantra will serve these times that "Hope is never lost" and the granting of wisdom will bring the Source of All Understanding. She named her daughters Faith, Hope and Charity and remains the Goddess of Wisdom incarnate.

The difference between the animal kingdom and humanity is that man is given a moral code via the knowledge of Religion. Whereas an animal injured is left to die as part of natural selection, man is required to neither harm, wound, kill, abandon or mistreat loved ones or strangers. Through charity, family, friends or the kindness of strangers one can survive in dire circumstances. Just as equally, one can be left for dead. Prisons are full. Domestic violence is out of control and systems are failing to protect women and children.

Although our Member of Parliament Justice Party, Derryn Hinch has beaten the odds by making public the names of convicted paedophiles, thereby alerting communities of possible danger to their children and perhaps embarrassing disclosures affecting their own family members. So finally law is protecting the victim rather than the rights of the perpetrator.

Disability has no guarantee of support in this life. Difference can be interpreted as a threat and the human cruelly ostracized or maimed further at any age and any stage.

I hated primary school. Fighting life-threatening bouts of asthma left me absent from school and in Grade 5 whilst playing with friends I overheard a comment which perplexed me from another girl to her friends,

"Don't play with her, she's going to die".

Six months previous I could not walk and my mother had to carry me to the bathroom. My ribs were visible. I had the same treatment as those with Cystic Fibrosis and on one visit from a Physiotherapist I collapsed after she thought it might be good practise to force me to run on the spot during an asthma attack. Mum asked her to leave and rang the Doctor who arrived in fifteen minutes with an Adrenalin shot. I had missed ¾'s of the previous year and even though I was a student selected to go to the next grade ahead of friends, severe and relentless asthma attacks had me bed ridden.

Over the dinner table that night I asked my parents if what the girl at Caulfield North Primary School had said, was true. Mum burst out crying and denied the prediction. I could see she was lying. Years later my father would say, "We nearly lost you". Out would come the handkerchief and he would blow his nose and wipe away tears.

Thankfully, I'm still here and so grateful to both my parents for their care. I accredit much of my interest in Art, Writing and Literature to a copious amount of reading material from both parents via library books and Dad's trips to Cole's Bookstore when he had his Chiropody practice in Swanston Street. Of course I was supplied with Art Materials as well. Noddy was a favourite, when younger and tales of faery enlightened an interest in mysticism. We were one of the first families to get a Box television and neighbours would pile in to stare at the magic. My brother and I would watch Shirley Temple movies and Laurel and Hardy Comedy together.

When stronger I attended Brownies which was a precursor to Guides where knot tying knowledge was shared. It did come in handy when tying a Houseboat to a tree one Christmas Holiday!

The good-bye ceremony at Brownies was held around a circle of water and connected to the "ancients of time" in witchcraft and architecture (The Parthenon). These were initial introductions to alchemy. It is serendipitous I was selected to play the role of one of the witches from "Macbeth" in Year 11 and cannot forget the lines to this day, "Double double toil and trouble, fire burn and cauldron bubble".

A simple bird-bath represents the wheel. It is a symbol of Faery Magic to be surrounded by a circle and a place of joy for animals both wild and domestic. It is a connection with divine souls and a gift of nature/ symbol of re-incarnation or metamorphosis through soul journey by sentient beings (including animals).

Brian Froud, in "The Faeries Oracle" states "To engage with Faery, stay open and let the faeries speak to you. Let them enfold you in faery light. If you desire an emotional or physical healing, direct that thought through the imagery to the light energy of the faery realm. Remember, as each man and woman is a microcosm reflecting the larger natural world, so healing of the Self is also a healing for the world. As above, so below."

"FAERY TALES" Rorschach Design (Psychological Perception) by Jill Rosier Astall

This is retro-cognition. An attempt to reach knowledge of the past via shamanism which is a practice that involves a practitioner reaching altered states of consciousness in order to perceive and interact with what they believe to be a spirit world and channel these transcendental energies into this world.

In the midst of a dilemma we are left fumbling in the dark. Plonked at the centre of a maze of differing potentialities, unclear of precise direction. Once mastered we can transform, metamorphose into a resplendent butterfly, fully formed and ready for flight. Akin to the reborn Phoenix, we are able to experience ethereal bliss within our mythical circle.

Brian Froud believes the Artist is shaman, journeying deep into uncharted inner worlds, then bringing back sensations and visions encountered in that mythic terrain.

When I paint I let the artwork speak to me, not literally though! Not one to hear voices. It dictates where it will go. I am in essence the messenger, transmuting creation. It is mystical and mythical. Quite often at the end of a session I will thank the painting. So that's where you wanted me to go! Sometimes in order not to dictate I will turn it upside down and am often amazed at the brains' ability to swap over domination from left hand side to right hand side.

Mystical empowerment is the most prized possession of all transcending the "chocolate box copyist style" of those without imagination. One other Artist in my Painters Group has faces appearing in her work after completion. As do I.

"FREAKY FOREST" Rorschach Calligraphy/painting by Jill Rosier Astall

Shamanism is harmony and balance with nature. Trees, plants and animals. Pollution brings despair. Culture is lost in survival and not joy or passion for life. Painting/Drawing/Writing and Music are a gateway to harmony, love and light.

"PEACE" Acrylic Painting/Digital Photography by Jill Rosier Astall

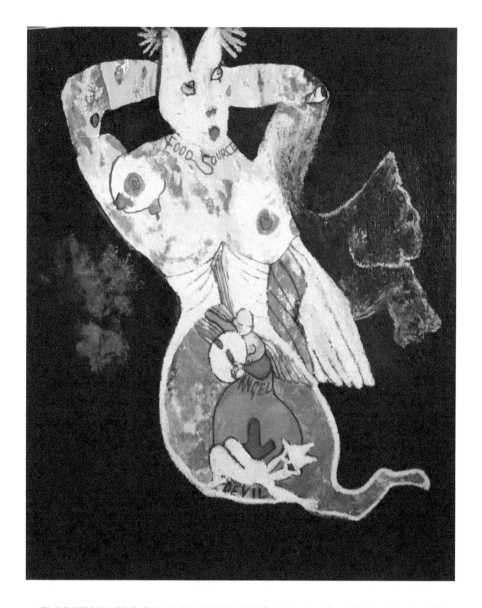

"MOTHERHOOD RORSCHACH" Painting by Jill Rosier Astall

The Rorschach "ink block test" is a psychological test in which subject's perceptions of inkblots are recorded and then analysed using Psychological interpretation, complex algorithms, or both. Some Psychologists use this test to examine a persons' personality characteristics and emotional functioning."

(Herman Rorschach, a Swiss Psychiatrist) cognition & personality, diagnosis of psychological conditions.

IMAGE 13 Calligraphy/Pen & Ink By Jill Rosier Astall

Shamanic sight is through their heart not eyes. It is Clairaudient and Clairsentient. Clairaudient is the supposed faculty of perceiving as if by hearing what is inaudible; Clairsentient is "clear feeling"; clear sensing" the ability to feel and experience the energy in an intuitive way and Clairvoyant a person who has a supernatural ability to perceive future events beyond normal sensory contact.

Various intuitives, mediums, psychics, sensitives or mystics have the capacity for one or more of the above divinations. The soul is a relentless representative of God. After you hear it once, you can never turn off that connection. Despite Religious xenophobia one does not require a monastery to be a mystic. Detachment offers a greater capacity to engage in life. Releasing all is acting with blind faith that you will hear, see or feel all meant to come to you. Give the entire situation over to God. Life is inter-dimensional. Being lifted into an altered state of consciousness, or parapsychology, is often experienced in meditation. Yesterday when deep in meditation I witnessed three shadows in front of me and at first found difficulty in deciphering who was what. Yellow glow was surrounding all figures and being transmuted back towards me directly to my heart. There was a figure in white to one side which appeared to be Christ. He was holding a baby and was filled with bliss and divine presence. There was another figure in white to the other side. This is presented as "The Holy Trinity", Father, Son and Holy Ghost. Christ did not appear as patriarchal but appeared to contain both energies of male and female. What happened next in my meditation stunned me. I left my own body on the couch and moved towards the feet of Christ. I held very tightly to the very end of his gown for what seemed like eternity but was probably five or so minutes. Again, as in my NDE experience, I did not want to come back.

My third parapsychology event was in 1996 around Christmas time and a festive time supposedly. All being well. Which it wasn't actually.

"I'll stay for Christmas." It said as it blithely put its family on the market. FOR SALE, the newly extended "home" and the wife and children to be sold as it were. Now a financial agreement of convenience but not agreeable or convenient really. Well, not for us.

A large, obvious statement for the neighbours was nailed to the picket fence I paid for out of my teaching superannuation. FOR SALE….one family and their home to swap for another.

The golden glow emitting from the light-globe was strangely romantic and comforting and a sign of power by men arranging stuff. I didn't feel grateful though, I felt "managed". Actually I'm still managed. There's a good girl.

Stuff was being arranged by husbands, lawyers, real-estate agents, the later clearly not impressed with having to deliver papers to a very close address five minutes away to a woman in a flat. Yes, very close. And yes, thank you I was aware of this situation, thank you for letting me know, I assured the nice agent.

As I snuggled up in my brass bed illuminated by the lovely golden light highlighting our forced sale, exhaustion swept over me. Too tired to worry, I drift off. Although a rather erratic pain to the left-hand side of my chest does not cease for a good twenty to thirty minutes and the right-hand-side of my temporal lobe still hurts from an "accident" not to speak of because apparently it didn't happen.

Wafting, I'm wafting towards His outstretched arms as I climb the Temple stairs. He's all in white, with a very long white beard. I am in awe of the magnificent temple, domed and pedestalled. Arms outreached he says, "You're safe now." I receive a hug from God himself. He has saved me from psychological and physical torture. Not scared here. Not threatened. Not an oversight, but valued and loved. How hard is it to return to the reality of life and the stranger calling late at night because he couldn't reach Lifeline to help his suicidal ideation. He has called the wrong number. I'm more likely to tell him to leave this world, having walked in the next one. There goes the chest pain again. I'm thirty-nine.

In "Experiencing the Shamanic Journey" tutorial the hidden world is rule. Reality is doubted. Images come from spirit world. Synchronicity happens, sometimes via "Mass Hallucinations" and altered states of consciousness or time travel. Shamanism is pure light not one Religion. It is not merely survivalist but attempts to keep spirit alive via communities coming together and manifests in the spiritual realm before the physical world. Look at people and see their strength, light and divinity. Don't send dark energy/don't transmute/don't participate in sorcery. Work through positive energy. It's who we become that changes our world.

A mystic necessarily returns to the world to be of use to God by helping others. There is no point in not putting what you have learnt into practice. As a mentor you must live your life to serve others and incarnate your theology. Actions speak louder than words and silence still gets the message across. Your sole/soul requirement is to commit to being devoted to your inner authority to the divine.

Marshall vian Summers in "The Reality of Your Spiritual Family", a family that helps to raise you in your greater understanding of yourself states "here you are not born into their care, like you are your physical family, but instead they come to you".

"You encounter them. And they have great impact on stirring a deeper awareness within you, a deeper understanding and the deeper mind that God has placed within you – the Mind of Knowledge."

Spiritual families come to you. I recall watching "The Don Lane Show" in the second year of my marriage. Mum had died four years before and I missed her terribly. The guest Psychic had referred to the dead being capable of contacting via electrical equipment (telephone, Television, etc.). He referred to a spirit trying to make contact.

"No, she's not here, yes it was very quick, it was your head, yes."

My Mum had an Aneurism. Always wondered if it was her trying to connect. But she always said, "Don't look for me, I won't be here".

In 1971 Julian Burton wrote a thesis "A Bucket of Blood", in which Doctors refer to separation anxiety, bereavement and grief being the cause of memory recall which prompts visual and auditory hallucinations. He had an experience re: his mother appearing in the kitchen and she looked ten years younger. She smiled at him and then dissolved! She was wearing a pale blue gown which he later related to his sister who informed him of a shopping trip she had with Mum where she tried on the same blue gown.

I remember my mother taking me shopping to Ishka, buying me a caftan and dropping me back at my flat I shared with another Jill. That night Dad and my brother knocked on the door informing me of Mum's admittance to the Alfred Hospital. I always regret not going with her to see my aunt after shopping with her that day and the image of her driving away is forever embedded in my psyche.

After death comes the will. In "Chafen & Chafen Will Case" one son was ill and gave his estate to his son. His other son had a dream where his father in "ghost" state told him to look in his jacket where he subsequently found another will sewn into the lining as a note referring to equal distribution of his will to five sons.

In "The Afterlife Revolution", 1984 discussions of manifestation of soul and human beings not being awake to them state the experiences of Annie Streamer (CIA) and her husband. Annie died of a Brain Cancer in 2013 and manifested the re-emergence of a white butterfly in her home and in drawings. Her husband and Annie witnessed the presence of "greys" in early courtship and grew through the process of accepting their existence.

Dr. Callum Cooper – Part 1 "Raising the Presence of the Deceased cites within a 24 hour timespan there appeared the sighting of a ghost in Australia, after-death communications and deathbed apparitions.

The day my mother died I was in Warrigal visiting a friends' brothers' home. I felt the need to go home and as we were travelling through a rough downpour the car swerved effortlessly off the road and into a ditch. My friend said she was not steering the wheel. It floated seamlessly off the road. My mother had died at the same time.

Physicians and Nurses both report the sighting of mist coming out of a head post death. To cynics this can be rationalized as negative consequences causing separation anxiety.

50% of the grieving felt their loved ones presence after death. 50% said yes to sensing smelling them or calling out to them. After my father died I associated the appearance of a giant butterfly during Christmas, to the manifestation of my father's soul.

Greek Mythology and specifically Pandora's Box relates to the need to not open the box as it may unleash all terrors of the world.

Studies question paranormal belief, personal experience, hope and religious belief. Associations can be cited via the appearance of butterflies, white feathers, coins, being touched, lights and premonition of death.

ENLIGHTENMENT IS WHAT HAPPENS WHEN THERE IS NOTHING LEFT BUT LOVE

Indian Philosophy speaks of Transmigration and a view that an individual soul is reborn in another body after death. The passing of one soul to another body. The belief is that we are one another and some of us is to be found in some of all of us. When a man's body dies, some part of him lives on in those who survive him. Indian Philosophy differs from Buddhist in that death is not considered important or pain inflicted on others is not considered as abhorrent as in Christian or Buddhist religions. The latter avoids the production of pain in others to produce Freedom. Indian Philosophy supports the right to fight to obtain freedom. All are united that complete freedom is the only thing worth striving for.....complete freedom being maximum concern with minimum attachment. Freedom is not only logically possible but is actually possible.

Fatalism or, fate in itself, can predispose man to believing that nothing can control or change what is to be. Doubts and fears can sabotage our freedom. Complete freedom is the removal of Karma and finds a route to self-knowledge.

Plato said "Commitment to the highest good forms the philosophy of a culture"

The Platonic notion of human nature presupposed that man's nature was limited, that his perfection consisted in the control of the passions by the intellect so that the reasoned life was the best life, balance of the soul was of the essence and this balance was defined in terms both of the encouragement of the rational faculty and the discouragement of the appetites. When one had reached the state of balance so attractively described by Socrates in such dialogues as the Republic, there was no farther to go; one had reached the limits of man's capabilities.

Morality, the highest value for him, lies in the exercise of his reason and the subjugation of his passions. Nietzsche and Eckhart questioned the supremacy of moral values, beyond good and evil.

For better or worse, the ultimate value recognized by classical Hinduism is not morality but freedom. Not rationality in the communities interest but control over one's environment, control of others and physical sources of power. The self and exploration of such rises above the social machine. There is supremacy of control and freedom over morality for example, yoga and guru teachings. The power of mind over body. Buddhi and the manifestation of superior spirit. The Yogi, for example, seeks to pass beyond good and evil, having superior awareness, discrimination and the ability to decide and act appropriately in tough situations. Same with the Guru or spiritual advisor. Mastery of the curriculum is paramount, as is insight and superior awareness. A leader in India is seen to be a hero, saint and teacher and worthy of everyone's trust and allegiance.

"LISTEN TO THE SILENCE" Buddha Photo Acrylic Painting/Writing by Jill Rosier Astall

The universal and the individual Self
"Know thou the self as riding in a chariot,
The body as the chariot.
Know thou the intellect (buddhi) as the chariot-driver,
And the mind as the reins.
The senses, they say, are the horses;
The objects of sense, what they range over.
The self-combined with senses and mind
Wise men call "the enjoyer".
He….who is mindful and impure
Reaches not the goal,
But goes on to transmigration (rebirth).
"He….who is unmindful and impure
Reaches not the goal,

But goes on to transmigration (rebirth)

"He….who is mindful and ever pure,

Reaches the goal. From which he is born no more."

The Eternal indestructible Self (God's Image)

"The wise one (the self) is not born, nor dies.

This one has not come from anywhere, has not become anyone.

Unborn, constant, eternal, primeval, this one

Is not slain when the body is slain.

"More minute than the minute, greater than the great,

Is the Self that is set in the heart of a creature here.

One who is without the active will beholds HIM and becomes freed from sorrow-

When through the grace of the Creator he beholds the greatness of the Self."

(Katha Upanisad)

Study of the dialogue between Naciketas & Yama (the GOD of the World of departed spirits).

BONDAGE & KARMA

We are tied to natural objects that satisfy basic needs and biological drives. The world of the passions binds us because of the emotional tensions which result from lack of reciprocation as well as our own excesses.

The inner world of our own personal being binds us through psychological tensions resulting from lack of self-understanding manifested in irrational fears, partial withdrawal or rationalization. Man is at the mercy of his habits which bring security and achievement but deny freedom to explore.

A man who takes a wife becomes routine and his perceptions dull, he becomes inflexible to its new developments which constitutes bondage and he is unable to respond emotionally.

He loses his discrimination and power to act appropriately and incisively. Habit has dulled him therefore there is tragedy and frustration.

Therein lies "hedonistic paradox".

He finds success does not enlighten him. Nor does suffering and frustration.

We find full lifetimes of experience, continuing success and failure in abundance are still not a sufficient condition for complete freedom and something else is needed.

This brings distinction between Dharma (all else is part of oneself) and Moksa (Complete Freedom). Attachment breeds bondage and habits which control the self and limit freedom. We find a paradox between renunciation and resignation in that where the man of minimal concern is resigned, the free man has renounced. The resigned man doubts his ability to master circumstances and has little faith where the renounced man has faith in his ability not to exert power for gain.

Krishna's Philosophy encourages the development of mutual concern between oneself and another so that each can reach MOKSA. The realization of this kind of freedom appears to require a continuity of SELF through time or between selves across space.

Self-knowledge is a necessary condition for renunciation and eventual complete freedom. It is necessary to have knowledge of one's personality make-up, of one's capacities at a given moment, so as to choose the appropriate role within which to renounce and thus become free.

If freedom is possible, then people have it in their power to be concerned for each other lovingly yet disciplined, spontaneous and responsible. If freedom is worthwhile everyone has a stake in everyone else's advancement for to help another become more concerned for yourself is at the same time to help yourself become more concerned for him/her.

LET THERE BE PEACE AMONGST US

LET US VALUE EACH OTHER

LET US VALUE OUR LIFE ON THIS PLANET

BEFORE IT IS TO LATE